NATURE UNVEILED

40 Reflections on Experiencing God's Creation

JILL SMITH

ILLUSTRATED BY STACEY BARR

Jill has the refreshing gift of awe and wonder! In *Nature Unveiled* she continually invites us to be curious about all that is right in front of us and to let it open our hearts to God and His personal love for us. Her questions help us to wonder about our world, our own hearts, and the heart of God.

KATHY KOELLEIN, SPIRITUAL DIRECTOR OF DOVEHOUSE MINISTRIES | DOVEHOUSEMINISTRIES.COM

Jill Smith combines her knowledge of nature as a professional forester with her love for God and His creation to produce a book that is both informative and inspirational. She invites us to see through her eyes and open our hearts to the spiritual truth God reveals through plants, animals, and land. These forty devotions will forever change the way you see the world.

LORI HATCHER, AUTHOR OF *REFRESH YOUR HOPE: 60 DEVOTIONS FOR TRUSTING GOD WITH ALL YOUR HEART.*

Nature Unveiled is a thoughtfully intimate, 40-day journey that explores the intricacies of God's creation, and the myriad of ways we can see His fingerprints on our human experience in the natural world. Jill Smith seamlessly weaves the holy scripture of God's word with one of God's greatest gifts to us: nature. Within these 40 moments, you learn to pause, breathe, and feel the inspiration of God in every birdsong, leaf, flower, and sunset.

JOSIAH LOCKARD, ASLA, PA, REGENERATIVE LANDSCAPE DESIGNER, RESTORATION ECOLOGIST, AND LEED GREEN ASSOCIATE

NATURE UNVEILED

40 Reflections on Experiencing God's Creation

JILL SMITH

ILLUSTRATED BY STACEY BARR

DEXTERITY
dexteritybooks.com

Dexterity, LLC
604 Magnolia Lane
Nashville, TN 37211

Printed in the United States of America.

First edition: 2023

10 9 8 7 6 5 4 3 2 1

ISBN: 978-1-947297-80-7 (Paperback)
ISBN: 978-1-947297-81-4 (E-book)

Publisher's Cataloging-in-Publication data
Names: Smith, Jill M., author. | Barr, Stacey M., illustrator.
Title: Nature unveiled : 40 reflections on experiencing God's creation / written by Jill Smith and illustrated by Stacey Barr.
Description: Nashville, TN: Dexterity, 2023.
Identifiers: ISBN: 978-1-947297-80-7 (paperback) | 978-1-947297-81-4 (ebook) Subjects: LCSH Nature--Religious aspects--Christianity. | Devotional exercises. | Christian life. | BISAC Religion/ Christian Living / Devotional Journal Classification: LCC BT695.5 .S 2023 | DDC 231.7/65--dc23

Cover design and Interior design by Thinkpen Design
Cover photo/illustration Stacey Barr

DEDICATION

I dedicate this book to my mother, Sharon Anderson, who passed her love of nature on to me. Her constant source of encouragement and her "can-do" attitude toward everything has inspired me to try new things my whole life. Thank you, Mom, for always believing in and celebrating me.

MY STORY

Nature Day Camp served as my introduction to the beauty and adventure of the natural world. The summer after first grade I attended a weeklong camp at the Kalamazoo Nature Center, and I was hooked. I attended two more weeks before age ten, when my family purchased a pop-up camper and lot at Sandy Pines in southwest Michigan. We stayed in this tiny camper with its tiny bathroom, with a long walk to the community shower in flip-flops. Camping afforded me a newfound freedom to explore nature, so I learned to fish, swim, play tennis, drive a golf cart, get a playground wooden barrel to roll, and encourage a toad to jump to the finish line.

As I got older, I was first in line to sign up for summer camp. I went to Camp Merrie Woode and Camp Barakel. If there had been more opportunities to be in nature—and an endless family budget—I would have attended camps all summer long. I made friends, honed my archery skills, tasted sassafras leaves, and sang camp songs by an impressive bonfire. I didn't know it at the time, but being outdoors was a way for me to disengage from the world and engage the eternal. I found a stillness not available at home, and it connected deeply with my soul. God used these experiences of simplicity and beauty to tend to my heart.

I entered college with a love for biology and a far-fetched plan to become a park ranger. I earned a BS in environmental biology at Taylor

University and an MS in natural resources from Ball State University. I worked in urban forestry for two summers during graduate school, which later opened the door to my dream job of working at Warner Parks in Nashville, Tennessee. I loved educating the public on all kinds of nature topics, managing the forest, working with teens, and growing in knowledge of plants, animals, and the land.

In my sixth year as the urban forester, I became pregnant and chose to stay home, leaving a job I loved for a child I loved. During this time, I sought the Lord, and He ministered to me through His creation. When I attended a Women at Rest listening retreat at Fellowship Bible Church on October 4, 2003, God spoke to me about soaring birds and their strategy of rest. This encouragement spoke deeply to my tired and restless soul. I jotted down, "I'm not abandoning my passion, I'm leaving a job. Why cling to the gift? Cling to the Giver. God made the impossible possible. Why do you doubt that He will do it again?" I later went home and wrote the first devotion for this book.

Over the years, God would give me clear connections between nature and the Word of God, and I would sit and write. In 2021, a small art group was formed at The Gate Church that became more about the deep friendships of three women and less about art. Little did I know that one of those women would become the illustrator of this book. In January 2022, God gave me the word *finish* as an encouragement to complete the thirty-day devotional. I shared that dream with others and believed that He would help me.

I began writing, editing, sharing, and trusting. God put people in my path to equip and encourage me. I attended my first Christian Writer's Conference with my friend Elaine Gordon and got brave enough to request meetings from a new editor friend, Jeanice Birch, and a publisher. I kept finding the ground underneath my foot as I took that next step. I had a meeting with my publisher, Dexterity Books, in January 2023, and they wanted to publish the book but also wanted nine more devotions. I smiled and trusted God to provide, since it had taken nineteen years for the thirty-one I had written. One week later, the nine were completed. It seemed that the Lord was still making the impossible possible for me!

I reached out to Kathy Shaw, my former Warner Park Nature Center colleague and friend, to discuss ideas and to ask her to edit the science content. I then contacted my art friend Stacey Barr to see if she'd consider illustrating the book. I had not seen her art at that point, but I knew her heart. She loved nature and God, and in my heart it seemed a perfect fit. She later revealed her dream: since seventh grade she'd wanted to illustrate a book, but it was never the right time to pursue her passion. Completing this book with a dear friend and seeing both of our dreams realized is just like God. He makes beautiful things from our humble offerings and uses simple things to convey His great love.

I encourage you to step outside with an expectancy to see God. Whether you are walking your neighborhood or hiking a park trail, look for beauty and listen for Him singing over you. Nature is the backdrop of our world. If you bring nature's beauty into the foreground of your life, you will find treasures hidden in plain sight. He speaks volumes through the mighty and the tiny. Slow your pace, observe the beauty, and pause to smell the roses so that you can see and feel the nearness of God. This display of beauty is purposeful to draw and connect your heart to His.

I ENCOURAGE YOU TO STEP OUTSIDE WITH AN EXPECTANCY TO SEE GOD. WHETHER YOU ARE WALKING YOUR NEIGHBORHOOD OR HIKING A PARK TRAIL, LOOK FOR BEAUTY AND LISTEN FOR HIM SINGING OVER YOU.

TABLE OF CONTENTS

EPIGRAPH

"But ask the animals what
they think—let them teach you;
let the birds tell you what's going on.
Put your ear to the earth—learn the basics.
Listen—the fish in the ocean
will tell you their stories.
Isn't it clear that they all know and agree
that God is sovereign,
that he holds all things in his hand."

JOB 12:7-10, MSG

SOARING WINGS

But those who hope in the Lord will renew their strength.
They will soar on wings like eagles; they will run and
not grow weary, they will walk and not be faint.

ISAIAH 40:31

Escaping agendas, deadlines, and the needs of others to focus on God is restorative, and it looks similar to birds that are resting and soaring. Birds that flap their wings become tired—the same is true for us. God did not intend for us to flap constantly and live from our limited abilities. When we are still, we can know His power and operate from His endless strength. Rest refocuses our attention and refuels us for the journey ahead.

Raptors, like eagles, hawks, and vultures, climb hundreds of feet in the sky by riding rising pockets of warm air. For soaring birds to ride this geothermal elevator, they simply need to open their wings and circle the heat source. As birds make their exit, they continue to soar even as gravity pulls them slowly toward Earth. Yet to remain at great heights they must search for another thermal source or flap their wings. Large birds can use this migration strategy on long journeys to conserve energy and reduce time searching for food and water.

*Come to me, all
you who are weary
and burdened, and
I will give you rest.*

MATTHEW 11:28

In what circumstances do you find yourself more apt to flap than to rest? Have you made rest a priority in your life?

Watching a bird effortlessly circle the sky is beautiful. Though vultures have a bad reputation for being scavengers, they are graceful and beautiful when they soar. They draw the attention of other soaring birds from miles away to join the ascent.

Vultures and hawks alike will soar and circle the same geothermal source without concern for one another as they rest and ride along.

Rest becomes contagious when the result is fresh strength. Others notice when you approach life with a fresh perspective, a renewed commitment, and a positive outlook. Modeling a lifestyle of rest encourages others to do the same. In Psalm 46:10, David pairs stillness with knowing God. It is in a posture of stillness that you are able to see Him more clearly.

In your stillness and pursuit of God, which is a greater struggle: quieting your mind or relaxing your body? What do you do to prepare to receive His love?

Still your mind and body and cease striving so that you can know God.

Additional Verses: Exodus 19:4, 33:14; Psalm 62:1; Matthew 11:28; Luke 5:16

NOTES

WHEN WE ARE
STILL, WE CAN
KNOW HIS POWER
AND OPERATE
FROM HIS ENDLESS
STRENGTH.

THE MOON

For now we see only a reflection as in a mirror; then
we shall see face to face. Now I know in part; then
I shall know fully, even as I am fully known.

1 CORINTHIANS 13:12

Our views of God, man, and our circumstances are limited in this life because we are only able to see and understand in part. God rarely reveals the whole picture to us but instead brings clarity over time. Sin committed against us and sins we have committed complicate how we perceive God. Our perspective of life must be through the lens of God's faithfulness and love toward us even when we do not fully understand.

Our perspective of the moon is also positionally limited, because the Earth and the moon orbit the sun in tandem. The moon rises in the sky at various times, sometimes during the day but often at night, and reveals its lit phase. Sometimes the moon's face is fully or partially lit and sometimes not at all. The moon, however, is never fully revealed because half of the moon is constantly turned away, so from Earth we never view its mysterious dark side.

Are you encouraged or discouraged by your limited perspective? Does the mysterious nature of God intrigue you or frustrate you?

In ancient times, a solar eclipse would strike great fear in people because they did not understand why the sun was turning dark. Now we know that this phenomenon is caused by the alignment of the Earth, the moon, and the sun, and we look forward to this celestial event.

A limited perspective can bring discouragement. In Psalm 42, we are encouraged to place our hope in a God who can see our past,

The lot is cast into the lap,
but its every decision is from the Lord.

PROVERBS 16:33

present, and future. He not only can see the outcome of every dream and every hardship, but He is also sovereign over them. Just as deeper understanding allowed peace to replace fear concerning a solar eclipse, the Holy Spirit and the Word of God give a new perspective on everything. Though we only see in part, we are promised that one day we will fully know as we are fully known.

Are you excited to see the veil removed and to see the hand of God in every aspect of life? What do you think Heaven will be like?

Though our knowledge is limited, we have a trustworthy God who is good.

Additional Verses: Job 42:2; Psalm 42:5; Proverbs 16:33

NOTES

THOUGH OUR
KNOWLEDGE
IS LIMITED,
WE HAVE A
TRUSTWORTHY
GOD WHO
IS GOOD.

KUDZU

We demolish arguments and every pretension that sets
itself up against the knowledge of God, and we take
captive every thought to make it obedient to Christ.

2 CORINTHIANS 10:5

O ur minds regularly spin with all kinds of random thoughts and ideas. Some of these thoughts can seem harmless at first but become deeply seated over time. A wayward thought might grow to alter the landscape of your mind if given permission. Thoughts are powerful, and when they are contrary to the thoughts of God, they can do great damage.

Unmanaged thoughts are as problematic as kudzu vines. Kudzu, a non-native invasive vine, is known as the plant that ate the South. Though initially introduced to the United States both to feed livestock and to combat soil erosion, it is now considered a devastating pest due to its fast-growing nature. Kudzu outcompetes native vegetation, easily overtakes large trees in search of sunlight, and alters its new habitat by shading out and destroying the plants it dominates.

When a wayward thought crosses your mind, do you recognize it? Are you able to uproot it so that its power over you is neutralized?

Kudzu is native to several Asian countries where it is naturally

Test me, Lord, and try
me, examine my heart
and my mind;

PSALM 26:2

controlled by diseases, insects, and other consumers. Displaced from its native habitat, kudzu grows rapidly (up to a foot per day) and spreads to new locations by birds that consume and disperse its seeds. Removing kudzu from someone's property is feasible if the few vines and roots are dug up and the homeowner remains vigilant.

Invasive plants and wayward thoughts must be identified and removed. God has instructed us throughout the Bible to set our minds, make up our minds, turn our minds, and examine and renew our minds because our minds are constantly processing information. As vigilant gatekeepers, our thoughts must be managed, or they will rule us. When our minds are controlled by the flesh they are hostile to God, but when our minds are controlled by the Spirit we have life and perfect peace.

Is your mind peaceful and focused on Him? Does the Holy Spirit have unrestricted access to your thoughts?

The next time you feel tangled and smothered by a wayward thought, remember that life and peace are promised when you give the Holy Spirit permission to remove it.

Additional Verses: Psalm 26:2; Isaiah 26:3, 55:8-9; Romans 8:6, 12:2; 1 Corinthians 14:33; Philippians 4:6-8; 1 Peter 5:7

THOUGHTS ARE
POWERFUL, AND
WHEN THEY ARE
CONTRARY TO THE
THOUGHTS OF GOD,
THEY CAN DO
GREAT DAMAGE.

OBEDIENCE

FISH

Put out into deep water, and let down the nets for a catch.

LUKE 5:4

The professional fishermen of Luke 5 approached the water expecting to catch fish. With mended nets, they sailed and rowed to their favorite locations and cast their nets into the deep. Over and over, they found their wet, heavy nets empty. Exhausted, they rowed back to shore discouraged and empty-handed. Their knowledge, experience, and patience did not equate to the catch they anticipated.

Some fishermen are drawn to the water to gather food, others to seek out a trophy, and still others to leave the worries of the shore behind. Dropping a hooked line in the water does not require much skill, but learning to catch fish requires the right equipment and knowledge, and an abundance of patience.

Have you experienced the disappointment of "casting a net" only to find it empty? Did you cease pursuing or did you persist through the discouragement?

Understanding the behavior of the local fish increases the likelihood of catching them. Not all fish are caught with a worm and a hook. Fish have different diets and strategies to evade predators, and they

Why, my soul, are you downcast?
Why so disturbed within me?
Put your hope in God,
for I will yet praise him,
my Savior and my God.

PSALM 42:11

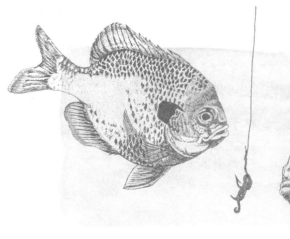

live at varying depths. Fishermen use their understanding of fish to entice them into their net, trap, or hook.

In Luke, the unsuccessful fishermen returned to the sea because Jesus, the teacher on the shore, sent them out. Though they did not catch a single fish all night, they loaded their boat and returned. To their great surprise, they experienced a miracle. Their nets were so full of fish that they had to recruit help to haul in the catch. Generally, the nets we cast have nothing to do with catching fish. Our nets are made from the knowledge and experience we have acquired to navigate the challenges of life. We pursue relationships and goals, and despite our best efforts, the nets can return with trash or nothing at all. God does not give us permission to pout and despair but calls us to cast the nets again.

Do you believe that God can perform a miracle in your life? Will you be obedient to cast the net into the deep once more, trusting God for a miracle?

When the expected outcome falls short, trust that God has an unseen plan that may require your obedience.

Additional Verses: Psalm 42:11; 1 Samuel 15:22; Matthew 9:20-22; 1 Corinthians 13:4-7

NOTES

WHEN THE
EXPECTED
OUTCOME FALLS
SHORT, TRUST
THAT GOD HAS
AN UNSEEN
PLAN THAT MAY
REQUIRE YOUR
OBEDIENCE.

STORM DEBRIS

Man looks on the outward appearance,
but the Lord looks on the heart.

1 SAMUEL 16:7, ESV

When God chose David to be the future king of Israel, He did not select David based on his standing with men, his accomplishments, his stature, or his age. From a human perspective, this caretaker of sheep did not look the part. God saw past David's unmanicured exterior to see his pure heart and warrior spirit, which were more valuable to God.

Forests are often left wild and unmanicured. Rain-drenched soil and strong winds can topple canopy trees, leaving messy piles of trunks, branches, and root balls scattered throughout the forest floor. In a protected natural area, these downed trees are left wherever they fall and are only cut from the roadways and trails to allow passage. In a manicured park or botanic garden, these fallen trees are cut up and hauled away to preserve the picturesque views.

Who or what has influenced you to be polished and presentable to others? What is the downfall of focusing on your physical attributes?

Hauling away trees from a manicured park robs the nutrient recycling process and depletes the soil. Trees left on the ground,

Flee the evil desires of youth and pursue
righteousness, faith, love and peace, along with
those who call on the Lord out of a pure heart.

2 TIMOTHY 2:22

however, interface with a network of worms, insects, mold, bacteria, and fungi that convert plant waste into nutritional building blocks. Debris piles may look chaotic and unsightly, but left in place they will allow the decomposers time to replenish the humus layer needed for new life to awaken.

Jesus singled out the Pharisees because they placed more value on their outward appearance than on living an authentic relationship with God and man. Jesus called them blind guides and whitewashed tombs because they hid behind a well-constructed façade that concealed the stink of greed, pride, and death. Jesus told them to clean the inside of their cup and dish first, and the exterior would follow.

What relational barriers are created when you disguise your feelings and bolster your image? What freedoms do you experience when you are single-minded and focus your attention on pleasing only God?

Being authentic in the transformation of your mind, heart, and spirit invites others to be transparent along their journey too.

Additional Verses: Matthew 5:8, 6:24, 23:1:39; 2 Timothy 2:22; James 1:6-8, 4:8

NOTES

BEING AUTHENTIC
IN THE
TRANSFORMATION
OF YOUR MIND,
HEART, AND SPIRIT
INVITES OTHERS TO
BE TRANSPARENT
ALONG THEIR
JOURNEY TOO.

HEARTWOOD

Let love and faithfulness never leave you; bind them around your neck, write them on the tablet of your heart.

PROVERBS 3:3

You store captured experiences in your heart and mind as memories. In Mark 8:18, Jesus replied to the disciples by saying, "Do you have eyes but fail to see, and ears but fail to hear? And don't you remember?" Jesus used this moment to address the fear that seized the disciples' hearts. Instead of correcting them, He encouraged them to remember. Jesus had fed thousands on five loaves of bread, but at that moment His disciples had lost sight of their historical record with Him.

For a tree, history isn't a forgotten memory; it is recorded in its cells and integrated into its makeup. History is stored in the tree's heartwood as annual rings. When a tree is cut down, the cross section allows you to count the rings and age the tree. If you look closely at the rings, they will reveal the tree's life story. Generally, spring growth is separated by dark narrow lines of summer growth, but the width of the annual rings will vary based on whether the tree had optimal or stressful growing conditions. Though trees record their history in their trunk, they lack the ability to reflect, recall, and learn from their past as we can.

Lord, you are my God;
I will exalt you and praise your name,
for in perfect faithfulness
you have done wonderful things,
things planned long ago.

ISAIAH 25:1

Does your history with God get hijacked by fear of your present or future? What do you pray or speak over yourself to counter these thoughts?

Major life events are also recorded in the trunk of the tree. Physical markers are visible only in the part of the tree that was affected. Those markers might include lightning or fire or animal damage, branch growth or decay, burls, and healed scars. If the tree is cut above or below those markers, the historical clues would be unseen in that cross section.

Journaling is a great way to record your history with God. In moments of despair, you can retrace your steps, read your cries for help and His response, and recognize that His faithfulness to you was and is still present. Choose to view your present circumstances through a historical lens, and you will be reassured of His unchanging love. Our Father desires that we would not just take pen to paper but that we would write His love and faithfulness on the tablet of our heart, which cannot be erased.

Can you recount His faithfulness to you by listing major life events? Do you see a pattern forming in His character alongside your deepening trust in Him?

Trust Him in the present and for your future because He will always be faithful.

Additional Verses: Deuteronomy 4:9, 11:18-21;
1 Chronicles 16:12; Psalm 77:11; Isaiah 25:1

NOTES

CHOOSE TO VIEW
YOUR PRESENT
CIRCUMSTANCES
THROUGH A
HISTORICAL LENS,
AND YOU WILL BE
REASSURED OF HIS
UNCHANGING LOVE.

THE PLAN
CICADAS

As he went along, he saw a man blind from birth. His disciples asked him, "Rabbi, who sinned, this man or his parents, that he was born blind?" "Neither this man nor his parents sinned," said Jesus, "but this happened so that the works of God might be displayed in him."

JOHN 9:1-3

The blind man whom Jesus met in John 9 lived a life shrouded in darkness. He did not know why he was blind nor that he would receive a miracle. He had lived a life of want, isolation, humiliation, and pain. In a moment Jesus made him new, and he could see that there was purpose and meaning to the darkness. God did not love him less because he was blind, though others believed this falsehood. God's mysterious purpose and plan were finally unveiled—as they will be in our own lives, for He is at work in the dark.

Life in the dark describes the lifecycle of the cicada. These insects can spend up to 17 years of their life underground. Their story begins when a female slices a tree branch to deposit her eggs. The nymph stage will fall from the tree, burrow into the ground, and grow by drinking sap from tree roots. When maturity is nearly reached, the cicada will struggle through the dirt and ascend a nearby tree to begin

Rejoice in the Lord always. I will say it again: Rejoice!

PHILIPPIANS 4:4

its transformation. The ground-dwelling clothes, worn by the cicada, are molted to reveal folded, wet wings. As the wings elongate and become dry and stiff, the cicada is freed to fulfill its purpose in life.

What questions remain about your time in the dark? Would you ask the Lord to reveal any lies, associated with this time, that you still believe?

Cicadas can "sing" loudly using their tymbals, but while they are below ground, they are silent. Cicadas use this dark time to develop their tymbal structure and form their song. Emerging from the ground, they embrace their new mission, shed their dark past, and sing about their newfound freedom, for they were made to fly and sing.

We have been encouraged in Philippians 4:4 to rejoice in the Lord always. We, like the cicada, were made to sing with great joy and from a place of freedom and security. Rejoicing is a directive, not an option. We are asked to rejoice not because we feel happy, but because we know that everything about our present and future is in His hands.

Do you give thanks in all circumstances, or do you complain about your lack of control? When your gratitude increases, does your joy follow?

May praise ever be on your lips as you celebrate all that God is doing in your life.

Additional Verses: Isaiah 45:3; Mark 5:25-34;
1 Corinthians 2:9; 1 Thessalonians 5:16-18

NOTES

WE ARE ASKED
TO REJOICE NOT
BECAUSE WE FEEL
HAPPY, BUT BECAUSE
WE KNOW THAT
EVERYTHING ABOUT
OUR PRESENT
AND FUTURE IS
IN HIS HANDS.

GEODES

For out of the abundance of the heart the mouth speaks.

MATTHEW 12:34, ESV

Jesus came to earth clothed as a man. His exterior wasn't unlike our own, but as God in the flesh, He possessed a beauty within that drew the attention of both the wise and untrained. Even as a young man, Jesus confounded the wise with His words. The scholars prejudged His youthful appearance and were amazed to hear the depth of His understanding of spiritual truths.

The beauty of a geode is hidden within its unimpressive shell: an ordinary-looking rock that becomes extraordinary when broken open. Geodes often begin as hollow, rounded, volcanic rock. Over time, as water seeps into the void, it leaves behind minerals that accumulate on the interior walls. Crystals then develop in the hidden cavity to create beautiful formations that are only revealed when the stone is opened.

Whom have you wrongly prejudged based on their image or their word choices? Have you been surprised by the depth or lack of depth of their understanding of God?

The interior of the geode is dependent on water penetrating the surface and on the minerals dissolved in it. Without the presence of mineral-rich water, the void is unchanged. When minerals enter the stone, the void is resurfaced with colorful layers such as purple amethyst, clear quartz, and blue celestite. Though this process takes a great amount of time, the result is incredible beauty.

The void in our hearts is filled over time with all kinds of good and evil experiences. We store a collection of the things we see, hear, feel, and experience without understanding the impact that stowing

A good man brings good things out of the good
stored up in his heart, and an evil man brings
evil things out of the evil stored up in his heart.
For the mouth speaks what the heart is full of.

LUKE 6:45

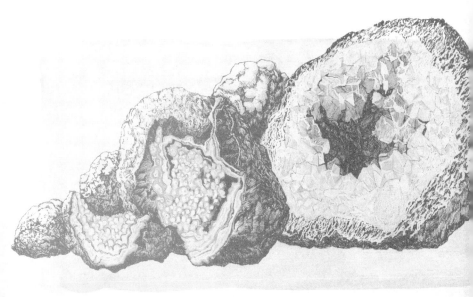

them will have on our lives. Since our mouths speak from the store-houses of our hearts, if a room is occupied with trash, the mouth will reveal its presence. However, if the room is filled with beauty, the mouth will sing.

What are you storing in your heart? Are you surprised by the words that come out of your mouth in times of stress?

Be a wise manager of the storehouses of your heart so that your mouth may reflect the great riches and beauty within.

Additional Verses: Psalm 49:3; Proverbs 15:14,28; Luke 6:45

NOTES

SINCE OUR MOUTHS
SPEAK FROM THE
STOREHOUSES OF
OUR HEARTS, IF A
ROOM IS OCCUPIED
WITH TRASH, THE
MOUTH WILL REVEAL
ITS PRESENCE.
HOWEVER, IF THE
ROOM IS FILLED
WITH BEAUTY, THE
MOUTH WILL SING.

COMMUNITY

FOREST FUNGUS

All the believers were one in heart
and mind. No one claimed that any of
their possessions was their own, but
they shared everything they had.

ACTS 4:32

The early Christian church focused on spreading the gospel of Christ and on living selflessly. They gave all they had to ensure that no one had unmet needs in their church body. The young church grew in knowledge by listening to the apostle's teachings, in faith while witnessing healing miracles, and in love as new believers joined the family of God. Their generosity was driven by their mission to share the treasure they had found.

Trees in a forest also generously support and strengthen their community. Scientists recently discovered that, far beneath the forest floor, where roots intertwine for stability, the trees send resources to support the health of individual trees in need. They share water, sugar, nutrients, and hormones, and can even send defense signals when they are under attack. This communal awareness keeps the entire forest healthy and strong.

Then the church throughout Judea, Galilee and Samaria enjoyed a time of peace and was strengthened. Living in the fear of the Lord and encouraged by the Holy Spirit, it increased in numbers.

ACTS 9:31

How does the early church's enthusiasm resonate with you? What keeps you from living more openhanded and more mission-driven?

The forest communication highway is not a construct of the tree's making but rather a symbiotic, or mutually benefitting, relationship forged with soil fungus. This fungus connects the root systems of all the trees in the forest and receives nutrition from the trees as its reward. This network allows the mother or hub trees as well as the entire network to send life-giving resources to the trees that are struggling to survive.

The Holy Spirit is the connector of our Christian community. He reminds us of those with needs, and He instructs us to pray and serve one another. When we respond to the promptings of the Spirit, we partner with Him to minister to the poor, the brokenhearted, the captives and prisoners, and those who mourn. The church is not a building but rather a community of believers who love and serve well.

Have you felt prompted by the Spirit to act on someone's behalf? Did you respond or did you question the calling?

God will prompt you and use you more powerfully as you respond consistently to Him.

Additional Verses: Isaiah 1:17, 61:1-3; Matthew 13:44-46;
Luke 12:48; Acts 2:42, 46-47, 9:31

NOTES

THE CHURCH IS
NOT A BUILDING
BUT RATHER A
COMMUNITY OF
BELIEVERS WHO
LOVE AND
SERVE WELL.

SWOOP OF A SWALLOW

Look at the birds of the air; they do not sow or reap or store away in barns, and yet your heavenly Father feeds them. Are you not much more valuable than they?

MATTHEW 6:26

Pausing with God during busy seasons provides a refueling rest. God will meet you in your need even if you only have a moment, because He is close and wants to be found. During busy seasons, pray for His strength, read or recite Scripture, or acknowledge His goodness to you. He longs for an extended time with you but is gracious to meet you in your immediate need. Isaiah 40 speaks of soaring but also reminds us of the walking and the running that take place in our lives. He gives us the power to not become faint when we walk and to not grow weary when we run. He sustains us when life is difficult and burdensome.

Swallows, like many of us, are busy. Swallows spend most of their day flapping their small wings to stay in flight because they are not equipped to soar like an eagle. Barn swallows fly chaotically around fields in order to capture hundreds of bugs daily. Their chase is beautifully hurried and filled with acrobatics, but they rarely stop to rest.

I will refresh the weary and satisfy the faint.

JEREMIAH 31:25

If, however, you examine one bird you will see that it flaps its wings a couple of times and then swoops or glides. Though their lives seem busy, swallows find moments of rest during their flight.

How do you stay connected to the Lord in busy seasons? What does your glide look like?

Birds spend most of their days (or nights) searching for food. They do not worry about their next meal because God provides for their needs. Though God grows food on trees, in fields, or in water, the birds must work to collect it. Life is filled with work, even for birds.

We too are responsible to work, but it is not our job to worry. Tasks can be divided into those that are required and those that are optional. Take an inventory of the jobs you are completing daily and ask the Lord if they are necessary or self-imposed. God will help you edit out the excess so that you feel less overwhelmed.

What tasks can be edited from your load? Are you willing to relinquish the optional tasks to someone else or to a future endeavor list?

Making extended time with God will reconnect you with His strength, remind you of His truths, and refuel your tank for the journey ahead.

Additional Verses: Isaiah 40:28-31; Jeremiah 31:25; Matthew 11:28-30

NOTES

GOD WILL MEET YOU
IN YOUR NEED EVEN
IF YOU ONLY HAVE A
MOMENT, BECAUSE
HE IS CLOSE AND
WANTS TO BE FOUND.

TRAIL HIKE

*Whether you turn to the right or to the
left, your ears will hear a voice behind you,
saying, "This is the way; walk in it."*

ISAIAH 30:21

Life is a journey full of obstacles, dangers, and intersections. Though God did not chart out our lives on a map, He gave us His Word and a knowledgeable trail guide, His Spirit, to lead us. Living by faith means that we also experience the mysterious ways of God. "Faith is the substance of things hoped for, and the evidence of things not seen (Hebrews 11:1, NKJV). Our faith grows in the "not seeing" times because we must rely on His guiding, leading, and voice for direction. By leaning into faith, we rely less on our ability to see and more on His ability to lead.

Clear directions from God help direct our steps, just as a map helps a hiker orient to a new trail system. When choosing a trail, hikers consider the land features, distances, and difficulty ratings. Then color-coded markers on trees or stakes keep them from getting lost, especially when trails intersect. With the help of a good map, they can account for many possibilities, except for common trail concerns such as poison ivy, fallen trees, and annoying insects.

Trust in the Lord with all your heart
and lean not on your own understanding;
in all your ways submit to him,
and he will make your paths straight.

PROVERBS 3:5-6

Are you a trailblazer or do you walk cautiously on a new trail? Does faith in God come easily for you?

On many public trails, park staff do regular maintenance so that hikers can focus on their beautiful surroundings and worry less about dangers. They might remove tripping hazards such as tree roots and rocks, add bridges and stepping stones, and clearly mark the paths. All of these alterations improve the trails for the traveler and make the journey more enjoyable.

God allows obstacles but promises to lead and accompany us along the path. By quieting our searching thoughts and active bodies, we posture our ears and our hearts to hear. Being still before God naturally leads to prayer and listening but also to a deepening faith as He navigates us around and through the obstacles of life.

What is your natural response to obstacles—discouragement or determination? Do you seek help or do you tackle the challenge alone?

Take comfort knowing that you are never lost or alone.

Additional Verses: Numbers 9:22-23; Job 23:11-12; Psalm 119:105; Proverbs 3:5-6, 16:9, 20:24; Isaiah 26:7, 42:16

NOTES

THOUGH GOD DID NOT
CHART OUT OUR LIVES
ON A MAP, HE GAVE
US HIS WORD AND
A KNOWLEDGEABLE
TRAIL GUIDE, HIS
SPIRIT, TO LEAD US.

SELECTIVE PRUNING

He cuts off every branch in me that bears no
fruit, while every branch that does bear fruit he
prunes so that it will be even more fruitful.

JOHN 15:2

God is involved in the day-to-day operations of our lives just like a vinedresser tending a vineyard. In this analogy, God is referred to as the gardener, Jesus the vine, and we His branches. When we remain connected to Jesus, fruit emerges in our lives as love, joy, peace, patience, kindness, goodness, faithfulness, gentleness and self-control (Galatians 5:22). To encourage a maturing faith and lasting fruit, God will prune away anything that hinders our growth.

Skill and artistry are needed to prune a tree well. Trees that receive this kind of intentional care are highly valued. As the tree grows, the caretaker assesses its health and considers the needs and concerns of the tree for its future. The caretaker will remove dead, diseased, and broken limbs and will prune away any growth that will not benefit the maturing tree. The goal of the caretaker is to create a beautiful, balanced, healthy specimen that will thrive for years to come.

What or whom has God pruned from your life recently? How has time changed your perspective of that event?

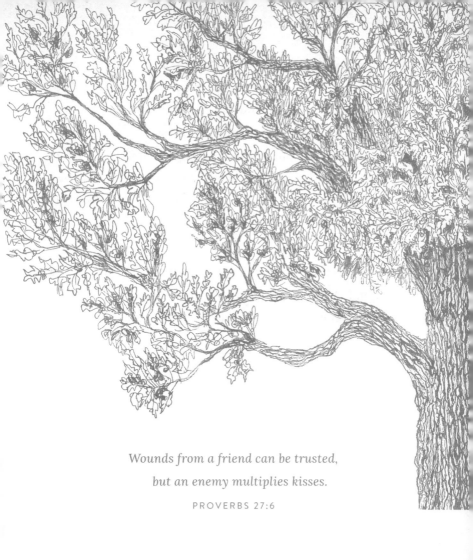

Wounds from a friend can be trusted,
but an enemy multiplies kisses.

PROVERBS 27:6

    The size of a pruning wound is relative to the age of the tree when it is pruned. Pruning wounds left on young tree saplings are small and heal quickly. When pruned, these young trees direct their limited energy toward growth that will benefit them long term. Delayed pruning is a detriment to maturing trees because the trees have invested in these wayward, diseased, or dying limbs. The resulting wound is often much larger and requires more time to heal.

Wounds from our God are not intended to kill us but rather to strengthen us. Wounds allow us to ask why, to seek Him, to grieve, to reconnect, to remember, and to see faith blossom. Trust that God's wounds are purpose-filled and will redirect our attention toward living more productive, fruitful lives.

Have you sensed God leading you to relinquish a dream or a relationship? Do you trust God fully to loosen your grip?

Trust that God's plan for us is much grander than anything we could dream up.

Additional Verses: Proverbs 27:6; John 15:1-17

NOTES

TO ENCOURAGE A
MATURING FAITH
AND LASTING FRUIT,
GOD WILL PRUNE
AWAY ANYTHING
THAT HINDERS
OUR GROWTH.

ARCTIC FUR

You prepare a table before me in the presence of my enemies.

PSALM 23:5

Impending hardship should not be a surprise to us. We have been promised that this world is full of troubles, and that we will encounter them often. The passage of 2 Corinthians 4:8-9 tells that we are hard-pressed but not crushed, in despair, abandoned, or destroyed. We are not devastated by our troubles because we have a God who foresees and prepares a way for us to endure and overcome.

Arctic summer and winter temperatures vary greatly, creating challenges for its residents. As daylight shortens or lengthens, arctic animals switch their camouflage colors in preparation for the approaching season. Photoreceptors measure the amount of daylight and trigger their bodies to produce either brown or white fur or feathers in preparation for the changing landscape. Their brown summer coloration helps them blend in with tree bark, branches, and leaf litter while white coloration helps them hide among snow-covered trees and ground. With a new appearance, wildlife adapt to the challenges of each changing season.

Were you ever prewarned of an upcoming season of difficulty? How did the Lord prepare you for it?

We are hard pressed on every side, but not crushed; perplexed, but not in despair; persecuted, but not abandoned; struck down, but not destroyed.

2 CORINTHIANS 4:8-9

As snowfall covers the ground, the arctic mammal's fur comes in white, thicker, and longer. Since this new fur lacks melanin, or pigment, air occupies the hair shaft; this adds another layer of insulation to keep the heat in and the cold out. Their fur protects them not only from the extreme temperatures but also from their predators. By blending in with their surroundings, they are able to search for food without the constant threat of attack.

David wrote Psalm 23 after experiencing both the pursuit of an enemy and the provision of the Lord. This beautiful depiction of the Lord tells of green pastures, quiet waters, and a banquet table in the presence of onlooking enemies. God does not prepare a table away from danger but in the middle of it. He is our provision, and the enemy does not dare approach.

Have you experienced provision from the Lord in the middle of trouble? Did God's provision come in the form of rescue, rest, His presence, a fellow sojourner or mentor, or something else?

Though trouble is ahead, look for how God is preparing a table before you.

Additional Verses: Song of Songs 2:4; Matthew 6:34; John 16:33; 2 Corinthians 1:3-4

NOTES

THOUGH TROUBLE
IS AHEAD, LOOK
FOR HOW GOD IS
PREPARING A TABLE
BEFORE YOU.

THE SUN

*Where can I go from your Spirit? Where
can I flee from your presence?*

PSALM 139:7

Just as the sun is positioned far from the Earth, God can seem far away at times. Yet God's actual presence is here among us. He created the world, dwells in it, and is actively involved in the lives of His creation. There is no place we can go where He cannot be found. In Acts 17, we are told that God was intentional about creating you. He desires that you would seek, reach out, and find that He is not far away. God wants you to find Him, so do not lose heart if you are still on that journey.

Life exists on Earth because its sun is 93 million miles away. The sun is a burning ball of gas with a surface temperature of around 10,000 degrees, so its proximity to Venus and distance from Mars makes these planets uninhabitable. Our sun is perfectly positioned for the Earth to sustain life because it consistently radiates the right amount of heat to warm the surface. The sun is reliable because it was created by a dependable and faithful God.

Are you on the hunt for God? Have there been times when you have questioned God's presence because He was hard to see or hear?

Come near to God and he will come near
to you. Wash your hands, you sinners, and
purify your hearts, you double-minded.

JAMES 4:8

From day to day, your experience of the sun differs. The Earth's axis tilts the planet toward and away from the sun, thereby creating seasons—the Earth leaning toward the sun in summer and away in winter. Cloud cover also alters our perception of the sun because it creates a visual and thermal barrier. The sun is consistent regardless of our experience of it.

You may seek God through an experience such as enjoying nature, singing, praying, reading His Word, or fellowshipping with others. He is near to us even when we don't feel Him close by. When we become sensitive to the presence of God, we can disregard the "weather" in our life that would otherwise change our perception of Him. Weather changes do not alter the sun, just as our trials do not alter our God. He is here even though our trials would tell us otherwise. God is always present and promises never to abandon us.

Do you recall a time of great need when you sensed God's nearness? Has that trial cemented your relationship in a new way?

Take heart—God is omnipresent, always with us.

Additional Verses: Genesis 28:16; Leviticus 26:11-12; Psalm 139:8-10; Acts 17:26-27; James 4:8

NOTES

THERE IS NO
PLACE WE CAN
GO WHERE HE
CANNOT
BE FOUND.

MISTLETOE

Jesus said, "Father, forgive them,
for they do not know what they are doing."

LUKE 23:34

Harboring unforgiveness is like hosting a parasite in your heart and mind. Unforgiveness will steal your joy and occupy your thoughts. Whether the offense is intentional, slight, or horrific, we are instructed to forgive, release the offender, and unchain ourselves. Jesus taught His disciples in Matthew 6 that receiving forgiveness was tied to and dependent on forgiving others. He spoke forgiveness from the cross even as He breathed His last breaths, modeling that even unto death, we too should forgive.

Mistletoe, like unforgiveness, steals resources from its host. Mistletoe is a parasitic plant that grows by thieving nutrients and water from its host tree. Its life begins as seed waste, left on a branch by a passing bird. With rain and sunshine, the seed germinates and sends a root into the branch. The root drills past the bark and finds the tree's live tissue, known as xylem, which flows with nutrients and water. Mistletoe quickly integrates into the tree's systems and is dependent on the tree for survival.

Do you forgive quickly or struggle to forgive? Were there role models in your life who forgave freely and lived in that freedom?

*Bear with each other
and forgive one
another if any of
you has a grievance
against someone.
Forgive as the Lord
forgave you.*

COLOSSIANS 3:13

Though the host tree drops its leaves in the winter, mistletoe remains persistently green because it draws its nutrition from its host. Though mistletoe is hardy, it cannot survive being disconnected from the host tree because it lacks the ability to draw water and nutrients from the soil. Once severed, mistletoe no longer steals the life of the host and begins to dehydrate and die.

Anger and bitterness die when forgiveness heals the heart and mind. In Genesis, we learn how Joseph did not allow unforgiveness to fester and stink up his countenance even after being sold into slavery by his brothers. Joseph forgave them and rose to power and wealth at an important time in history and not only saved the region from famine but also saved his family, who had wronged him. He extended grace and mercy to his family because he had already forgiven them.

Have you been able to forgive without keeping a record of wrongs? Is there someone, dead or alive, whom you need to forgive?

It is time to extend the forgiveness you have received, to others and to yourself, so that you can walk through this life unshackled.

Additional Verses: Genesis 50:15-21; Matthew 6:9-15,
18:21-22; Ephesians 4:32; Colossians 3:13

NOTES

HAVE YOU BEEN ABLE

TO FORGIVE WITHOUT

KEEPING A RECORD

OF WRONGS?

COVERING
BROOD

Whoever dwells in the shelter of the Most High
will rest in the shadow of the Almighty.

PSALM 91:1

The Psalms encourage us to hide, take refuge, and find shelter in the shadow of God's grandeur. He is referred to as one with wings like the parental bird. He is our protection in times of disaster and our help in times of need. When we dwell near Him, we find rest and relief from the pressures and hardships that swirl around us. We are invited to leave the chill of the world and receive His warm embrace.

Safety and warmth are found in the nest for both eggs and featherless hatchlings. A well-constructed nest provides safety from falling and protection from the wind, but the key to their survival is their parents' covering. During the nesting season, the mother (and sometimes the father) will lose a patch of feathers on their belly to expose their warm skin. This brood patch allows skin-to-egg or skin-to-skin contact so that heat is exchanged more efficiently to keep the young alive.

Were your earthly parents a positive or negative influence on you as you relate to God as your Father? Have you embraced or resisted being perfectly loved by Him?

Whoever fears the Lord has a secure fortress,
and for their children it will be a refuge.

PROVERBS 14:26

As the hatchlings grow feathers, they retain more of their own
body heat but are still dependent on their parents. Often the mother
and father team up to gather a constant supply of food for the growing
birds. As the parent swoops into the nest, the babies chirp and open

their mouths wide to signal they are hungry. The nestlings know that they are safe and so they loudly, but temporarily, make their needs known to their doting parent.

Maturing in the faith does not mean we launch into the world apart from the watchful, protective guardianship of God our parent. He invites us into the safety of His shadow, under His wing, in His rampart or castle whether or not we are threatened. We will never outgrow His parenting love for us!

Have you been raised to be a strong, independent person? What would it look like to be both a dependent child of God and a leader in the world?

You are covered and protected by a loving parent who will not fail you.

Additional Verses: Psalm 17:8, 31:19-20, 36:7, 57:1, 63:7, 103:13-14; Proverbs 14:26

NOTES

WHEN WE DWELL
NEAR HIM, WE
FIND REST AND
RELIEF FROM THE
PRESSURES AND
HARDSHIPS THAT
SWIRL AROUND US.

PERSISTENT RIVER

Whoever drinks of the water that I will give him will never be thirsty again. The water that I will give him will become in him a spring of water welling up to eternal life.

JOHN 4:14, ESV

God's Spirit is actively flowing in and through our lives. God takes the mystery of His Spirit and relates it to a simple liquid that we consume daily: water. We are dependent on water to live, and we are also dependent on the Holy Spirit to walk out the Christian life. Our soul receives refreshment from His Spirit—without it we walk around parched and empty.

Rain droplets infiltrate porous soil and seep deep into the ground to form an unseen river. Groundwater follows gravity and the path of least resistance as it navigates through permeable soil layers, between rocks, and through voids. When groundwater eventually trickles out of hiding, it feeds a surface waterway. Creeks become streams and grow to become rivers as they merge and build on their way to the ocean, their final destination.

In what ways do you perceive that the Holy Spirit is alive in you? Can you explain your transformation to others?

Flowing water can be halted. The Dead Sea, which is below sea

Be kind and
compassionate to one
another, forgiving each
other, just as in Christ
God forgave you.

EPHESIANS 4:32

level, has water flowing in but not flowing out. Water escapes this depression only through evaporation, leaving behind accumulated minerals that make the lake toxic to all life. Flowing water is critical to the life of the lake. Without it, the life within ceases to exist.

Unrepentant sin will quench the Holy Spirit's voice but is not always the reason He is quiet. Living out a wholly repentant life does not guarantee a keen awareness of God, for He is loud at times and quiet at others. But take heart, for God is active and moving even when we cannot perceive Him.

In what ways have you restricted the Holy Spirit from speaking in and through you? Are you willing to be used?

Hallelujah, you have a well of living water that will never run dry.

Additional Verses: Jeremiah 2:13, 17:13; John 7:37-39; Ephesians 4:29-32; 1 Thessalonians 5:19

NOTES

OUR SOUL
RECEIVES
REFRESHMENT
FROM HIS SPIRIT—
WITHOUT IT WE
WALK AROUND
PARCHED AND
EMPTY.

MATURING SEEDS

In their hearts humans plan their course,
but the Lord establishes their steps.

PROVERBS 16:9

A quiet mind serves as a seedbed for planning your next step. Plans originate from the ideas, desires, and intentions of the heart and mind but can also originate from God's call on your life. These ideas become the focus of our attention, our conversations, and our prayers, but they do not become realized without an action plan. It is the Lord who orchestrates the forward movement of our dreams, but sometimes they are torn down and rebuilt with new architectural plans.

A fertile ground receives the plant's potential in the form of seeds. Most plants reproduce and spread through the vehicle of seeds, and since it is preferable that seeds do not grow nearby and compete with the parent plant, many seeds are designed to travel. Lightweight seeds are transported by the wind, buoyant seeds are carried by water, and seeds with stiff hairs hitchhike on the fur of passing animals. Seeds that reach the ground are dependent on many environmental factors being favorable to grow and mature.

What plans are you considering right now? Has God given you

For no word from
God will ever fail.

LUKE 1:37

action steps to move forward or are you waiting?

Sequoia seeds thrive because of fire. Sequoia cones can lay protected on the ground for 200 years just waiting for a fire to ravage
the forest understory and open the cones. Likened to a time capsule,
the sequoia seeds are released when the forest is in need. By waiting

to germinate, the seeds receive sunlight and nutrition from the ash of the fallen, which allows these tiny seeds to grow into giant trees when the timing is right.

God invites us to dream the impossible because He can create a giant of a tree from a dream in our heart. We view life through experience and ability, but God broadens our vision and expands our mission. Partnering with God turns the impossible into the possible. The package, focus, or timing may not align with ours, but God brings clarity to the broader plan by revealing His heart to us. Resist the temptation to be discouraged if you have a dream but haven't seen the fulfillment of it quite yet. God holds the timetable and asks that you trust Him with it.

Do you spend time dreaming? Do you believe that God can do the impossible through you?

Be encouraged because with God all things are possible.

Additional Verses: Psalm 37:4; Matthew 19:26; Luke 1:37; Romans 8:25

NOTES

GOD INVITES
US TO DREAM
THE IMPOSSIBLE
BECAUSE HE
CAN CREATE A
GIANT OF A TREE
FROM A DREAM
IN OUR HEART.

LIGHTNING BUGS

*At one time you were darkness, but now you are light in the Lord.
Walk as children of light.*

EPHESIANS 5:8, ESV

Jesus brought light to a lost world, exposed the darkness, and drew people out of the shadows. People were drawn to Him by the hundreds because He was unlike anyone they had ever encountered. He was God in flesh and the light of the world. As we place our trust in Him, we are transformed into children of light. The light we hold, though a smaller wattage, shines brightly in dark places. When we radiate this light in the darkness, others see it and wonder about its source.

On dark summer nights, small flashes of light draw our attention. Lightning bugs communicate with their light, which they create from a chemical reaction in their bodies. The males flash their lights while flying and search for females who flash their lights from the ground. The males hunt for a specific light pattern that matches their own, to mate with the right lightning bug species.

Is your light shining for all to see or do you keep it hidden? Who introduced you to God, and what about his or her life drew your attention and piqued your curiosity about God?

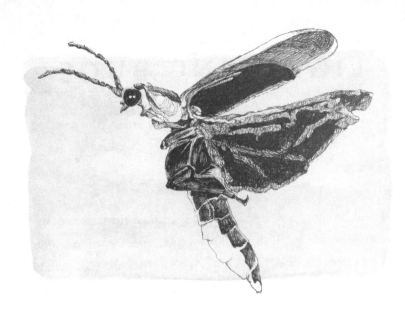

*But whoever lives by the truth comes into the
light, so that it may be seen plainly that what they
have done has been done in the sight of God.*

JOHN 3:21

Lightning bugs are toxic to most predators and therefore don't
need to hide. Males, however, can fall prey to female lightning bugs.
After the female mates with her kind, she can mimic the flash of a
different lightning bug species to lure a male from that species in as
dinner. She consumes this unsuspecting male to provide a boost of
nutrition for her growing eggs.

Similarly, our enemy can masquerade as an angel of light to lure you into sin. Do not be fooled by his schemes to deceive, for his aim is to kill and destroy. Prepare yourself for his attack, because it isn't a question of *if* he will attack but rather *when*. Be on guard, for he is a predator of man.

Are you different from the world? Do your actions and words prove it?

Do not be ashamed to offer what the world cannot, for you have the light of Christ within you. Let it shine for all to see!

Additional Verses: Matthew 17:1-2; John 3:21,
12:46; 2 Corinthians 11:14; 1 John 1:5-7

NOTES

WHEN WE
RADIATE THIS
LIGHT IN THE
DARKNESS,
OTHERS SEE IT
AND WONDER
ABOUT
ITS SOURCE.

FARMED LAND

There is a time for everything, and a season for every activity
under the heavens...a time to plant and a time to uproot.

ECCLESIASTES 3:1-2

The hardpan soil of our heart can grow firm and crusty with old ways, thoughts, and desires. To break up the soil, the Holy Spirit plows the old and replants the new to make us more like Jesus for use in His kingdom. If you are willing, He will act in and through you to bring His heart to the world. Allow the plow to break up new ground so that He can cast new vision in your heart.

The farmer's plow breaks up sunbaked clay, buries weeds, and brings rain-leached nutrients to the surface. Soil preparation protects the newly planted seeds from predators and heat by nestling them inside the disturbed soil. The exposed soil also grants the seeds better access to water and nutrition for their start in life. Farmers invest their time and labor into the land with the hope of a bountiful harvest.

What old ways do you battle to keep in your new life? What is the mission you have been assigned by God?

Farmland left fallow, or unworked, can rest. The fallow land is not inactive but rather in a state of rebuilding. Plants that grow during a fallow period are left to degrade, which adds organic matter to the

Ephraim, what more have I[a] to do with idols?
I will answer him and care for him.
I am like a flourishing juniper;
your fruitfulness comes from me.

HOSEA 14:8

depleted soil. Beneficial bacteria increase in number, break down plant debris, and contribute to creating better soil structure with less compaction. By leaving land fallow for a season, farmers increase the yield of future harvests for years to come.

After the Holy Spirit works in and through you, you may need a time of rest or a sabbatical. This is not an unproductive time with God but rather a time to refuel, refocus, and dream. You have physical, emotional, and spiritual limitations that cannot be ignored. Pouring into others can leave you empty if you are not careful to attend to your own needs. There is a season for everything under heaven, including a time to work and a time to rest.

When was the last time you took a weekend of rest with the Lord? How did that time change your outlook on the future?

A season of work and a season of rest both have great value for your growth, so trust in the timing, correction, and instruction of the Lord.

Additional Verses: Isaiah 28:24-26, 61:11; Hosea 14:8; Matthew 13:1-23; Philippians 2:12-13

NOTES

THERE IS A

SEASON FOR

EVERYTHING

UNDER HEAVEN,

INCLUDING

A TIME TO

WORK AND A

TIME TO REST.

STRENGTH
CLIMBING VINES

Those who wait on the Lord shall renew their strength.

ISAIAH 40:31, NKJV

The word *wait* in Isaiah 40:31 comes from the Hebrew word *qavah*, which can be translated to "bind together." This word is also translated as to "wait for," "hope in," "wait upon," and "trust in." The process of waiting, hoping, trusting, and binding is like the life of a Christian, as well as the life of a vine. The vine needs to be bound to another structure just as we must be bound to God.

Young climbing vines lack rigidity and strength, so they grow horizontally in search of a vertical object. Once found, vines use their arm-like appendages, called tendrils, to grasp another plant or structure. The cells in the tendril respond to touch, wrap around the structure, and tighten their coil to butt the vine against the object so that it has the support needed to climb upward. New tendrils are produced along the vine to grasp more structures, giving it a competitive advantage for sunlight over the plants on the forest floor. Though rooted in the ground, with time and persistence, vines will grow vertically.

What does your "wait" look like? Do you battle impatience in your discontent?

*Be still before the Lord
and wait patiently
for him; do not fret
when people succeed
in their ways, when
they carry out their
wicked schemes.*

PSALM 37:7

Climbing vines that grow along the ground and never find another object to climb lack a competitive advantage on the forest floor. In a forest ecosystem, light reaching the ground is restricted as it filters through the tree and shrub layers. Unless vines find a structure to climb, they often will not have enough stored energy to produce flowers, fruit, and new branches, thereby limiting their growth potential.

Relying solely on ourselves can be exhausting and fruitless. Our bodies, minds, and abilities are restricted by our strength. It is not until we fully rely on God that our ability to overcome our limitations is revealed. God provides strength to the weary and worn down because He has an endless supply. We are to be still before the Lord and wait patiently for Him because it is His strength that renews our confidence and restores our joy.

Where do you need fresh strength right now? What fruit have you seen born from the spiritual discipline of waiting?

You are a choice vine planted by God, and He promises to provide the strength you need when you offer Him your trust.

Additional Verses: Psalm 37:7,24, 40:5; Isaiah 30:18, 64:4; Jeremiah 2:21; 1 Corinthians 2:9

NOTES

WE ARE TO BE
STILL BEFORE THE
LORD AND WAIT
PATIENTLY FOR
HIM BECAUSE IT
IS HIS STRENGTH
THAT RENEWS OUR
CONFIDENCE AND
RESTORES OUR JOY.

REALIGNMENT
PREENING

Create in me a clean heart, O God; and
renew a right spirit within me.

PSALM 51:10, KJV

Examining your heart before the Lord may reveal misaligned thoughts. When you believe the lies of culture, of your enemy, or even of your own skewed thoughts, you leave yourself vulnerable to further attack. By realigning to truth, you reconnect with the Lord and His power to expose lies, shield you from attack, and strengthen your inner self.

Birds preen their feathers to keep them clean, aligned, and ready for flight. Feathers are composed of barbs and barbules that hook onto each other, but when the feathers get disturbed, the barbs are pulled apart, creating a gap. For flight feathers to perform well, the birds run their beak or toe through each feather to reattach the barbs and close the gaps.

Have you felt battered from the circumstances of life? Do you spend time realigning to truth, or are you rehearsing lies from your enemy?

Preening also involves using oil and removing "hitchhikers"—ticks and mites that feed on the bird's blood and feathers. The preening process removes tiny carriers of disease and keeps the bird healthy

*May these words of my mouth
and this meditation of my heart
be pleasing in your sight, Lord,
my Rock and my Redeemer.*

PSALM 19:14

and agile for flight. Birds also use oil to condition their feathers, to prevent them from becoming brittle, and to repel rain and lake water. This helps insulate their skin and regulate their body temperature.

Keeping your heart tender to the Lord means that you are postured to receive both healing and correction. If your heart is misaligned, pray that the Lord would reveal the root cause. Like the ticks and mites that want to hide and feed on the bird host, sin also wants to remain hidden to destroy you and disconnect you from the Father. The Holy Spirit will expose sin and give you the power to overcome its grip on you. When preened and ready for flight, you will live in a freedom that the world cannot offer.

What sins keep you from experiencing an abundant life? Are you resistant to correction or do you welcome it?

God's kindness draws us to correct course and realign with His heart, so listen for His gentle Spirit's lead.

Additional Verses: Psalm 19:14, 103:12; Romans 2:4

NOTES

GOD'S KINDNESS
DRAWS US
TO CORRECT
COURSE AND
REALIGN WITH
HIS HEART, SO
LISTEN FOR
HIS GENTLE
SPIRIT'S LEAD.

TRADE WINDS

Then we will no longer be infants, tossed back and forth by the waves, and blown here and there by every wind of teaching and by the cunning and craftiness of people in their deceitful scheming.

EPHESIANS 4:14

The Bible is the source of all wisdom and only flows in one direction: from His heart to ours. Reading the Word of God opens the door for the Holy Spirit to speak. He will use the words on the page and give us insight and direction for our own lives. God also raises men and women to teach the body of Christ and to equip us for life and ministry. We are cautioned, though, that some will claim to know God but are false teachers and deceivers. We must be readers of the Word so that we can discern between truth speakers and false teachers.

The wind is ever-changing and blows on its own schedule. We can detect its presence by feeling the breeze or witnessing the movement of objects. There is a type of wind, however, that is predictable and reliable year-round—always moving from east to west and found just north and south of the equator. This consistent force is created because of the rotation of the Earth as well as temperature and pressure gradients. These winds were coined "trade winds" because they

So then, just as you received Christ Jesus as
Lord, continue to live your lives in him.

COLOSSIANS 2:6

made trade between continents possible. Ship captains still chart their paths using trade winds because they quicken their long journeys.

In your desire to believe, have you been led astray by a false doctrine? What was the red flag that alerted you to the falsehood?

Wind generally is not consistent in speed or direction. The ascending warm air and descending cold air bring wind, clouds, and sometimes precipitation. Wind's seemingly random intensities and directions affect both the living and the nonliving, but one plant in particular benefits from this erratic pattern: it is the Russian thistle or tumbleweed. As the plant tumbles here and there, it drops its seeds across the desert landscape. The wind determines the locations of future thistle plants.

Infants of the faith can be tossed about by the prevalent voices of culture to think and act as prescribed. Culture has its own ideas about the human condition and offers solutions that may be in opposition to God's Word. We are to be rooted and grounded in the Word so that we are not swayed to accommodate the world.

What does being rooted and grounded in the faith mean to you? What cultural ideas have muddied your faith?

The Word of God, like His nature, does not change.

Additional Verses: Ephesians 3:16-19, Colossians 2:6-8, Titus 1:10-16

NOTES

WE MUST BE
READERS OF THE
WORD SO THAT
WE CAN DISCERN
BETWEEN TRUTH
SPEAKERS AND
FALSE TEACHERS.

GRAFTED TREES

*Submit to one another out
of reverence for Christ.*

EPHESIANS 5:21

Close relationships often cause injury, leading to either division and self-protection or a deeper connection through mutual understanding. Our deepest wounds often come from our families. We are vulnerable to injury when expectations are exposed and feelings are unmasked. Pride is often the obstacle that keeps many of us from mending these relationships and giving priority to the other's view. By approaching each other with humility, hearts open and healing can begin.

Trees that embrace the wounds of another grow to become stronger because of their union. Grafting fuses two trees into one either through a natural or man-made process. The husband-and-wife tree is the result of a natural graft. New England tradition speaks of newly married couples planting two trees close together. When they incur bark damage on windy days, due to their proximity, they will heal joined together. Over time, they exchange their independence for connection as they become one in both function and appearance. Another grafting example is when two trees are selected with strengths

As iron sharpens iron,
so one person sharpens another.

PROVERBS 27:17

that offset the other's weaknesses. The strengths of these trees are used to create one strong desirable tree.

Have you constructed walls to keep others from injuring you? What do those walls look like to you and to them?

Fruit trees and vines are often artificially grafted together to create strong plants and an expected yield. A branch from a delicious fruiting tree may be combined with a tree root that tolerates extreme temperatures or resists disease. Both trees must incur an injury for this relationship to work. The healed injuries cause these trees to produce a better harvest grafted together than they could create separately.

We were designed for relationships that sharpen one another just as iron sharpens iron (Proverbs 27:17). Accountability, vulnerability, and a boldness to love with both encouragement and correction are important elements of journeying together. When the weaker members of the body of Christ grow stronger, the entire community does as well.

Are you sharpening those around you? Do you permit others to sharpen you?

You need others just as they need you, so do not journey alone.

Additional Verses: Proverbs 27:9,17, 17:17; Romans 11:11-24;
1 Thessalonians 5:11,14; Hebrews 10:24-25; James 5:16

NOTES

YOU NEED
OTHERS JUST
AS THEY
NEED YOU,
SO DO NOT
JOURNEY
ALONE.

JOY

PLAYFUL COYOTE

The Lord has done great things for us, and we are filled with joy.

PSALM 126:3

Happiness and joy are used interchangeably in conversation, but they are different. We experience happiness when life's circumstances are good, but it evades us when challenges arise. Joy is a gift to the believer and a fruit of the Spirit of God and therefore is not dependent on a feeling but rather on our relationship.

Happiness exists in the animal world, but joy is limited to God's children. Coyotes exhibit feelings of happiness, curiosity, and playfulness as they navigate their habitat. These interesting creatures belong to the canine family, so they share many dog-like characteristics. As opportunistic omnivores, they eat a variety of fruit, insects, and animals. They are known to leap and bound around a field of tall grass while hunting prey as if it were a game. They also play with their food, as a dog would a toy, and toss it in the air before consuming it. Coyotes appear to enjoy their life in the wild.

Are you riding the emotional roller coaster of life, or do you experience an emotional steadiness that transcends your circumstances? Can you be both joyful and authentic?

Happiness is a temporary emotion that can be replaced by pain.

You make known to me the path of life;
you will fill me with joy in your presence,
with eternal pleasures at your right hand.

PSALM 16:11

Generally, animals that are injured hide from predators and remain quiet until their bodies heal. Their normal pursuits become shelved as they focus on protecting themselves from further harm. When healed, happiness may return as they resume running and hunting.

Joy can persist in the presence of pain. Jesus modeled this on the cross. Hebrews 12:2 tells us that Jesus endured the cross for the joy He knew was coming. He fixed His joy on the result of the struggle— demonstrating to us that joy can be experienced despite encountering great despair. Losing sight of our hope disconnects our joy and puts the emotion of the day on center stage. Joy is not an emotion but rather an indicator of a deep well filled by a limitless God. Christians should be distinguished from the worry and despair of the world by revealing an abundant life that is "joyful in hope, patient in affliction, faithful in prayer" (Romans 12:12).

What or whom is the thief of your joy? How can you protect your joy from being stolen?

You have been promised an eternity with God, so rejoice!

Additional Verses: Nehemiah 8:10; Psalm 16:11, 51:12, 126:2-3; Hebrews 12:1-2

NOTES

JOY IS A GIFT TO
THE BELIEVER AND
A FRUIT OF THE
SPIRIT OF GOD
AND THEREFORE IS
NOT DEPENDENT
ON A FEELING
BUT RATHER ON
OUR RELATIONSHIP.

HIS IMAGE
CLAY

Like clay in the hand of the potter, so are you in my hand.

JEREMIAH 18:6

When God created the world, He used the dust of the Earth to form Adam. Job understood this well when he said, I am just like you before God; I too am made out of clay (Job 33:6, NCV). God created man and woman in His image, and they were and still are the pinnacle of His creation. We are the work of His hand, formed and fashioned in His likeness and lovingly stamped with His maker's mark.

Clay proves to be a source of frustration for the gardener but a delight for the potter because of its physical properties. Clay particles are so tiny that a single grain must be viewed under a microscope. When found en masse, these grains fit so tightly together that they restrict the movement of water. Other soil components, like silt and sand, are much larger and bind together loosely, allowing water to flow through them freely. Clay, silt, and sand are often found mixed in varying percentages and are collectively referred to as soil.

Have you spent time working with clay or building with sand? Are you amazed at the beauty of God's creations made from the dirt of the earth?

Then the Lord God formed a man from the dust of the ground and breathed into his nostrils the breath of life, and the man became a living being.

GENESIS 2:7

A lump of clay brims with potential. It can become something useful or beautiful, revealing the artist's ability. In the hand of a novice potter, the final product may disappoint. But for a skilled artist, the pliable clay transforms into the master's intended design. The master potter's artistry is limitless when turning clay into a vase, bowl, or plate of any size, shape, color, or design.

Our God is a master potter and has created us with skill, intention, and great love in the womb of our mothers. He only creates masterpiece vessels to house His Spirit, and so we are walking, talking jars of clay carrying an all-surpassing power. We may not like our shape or our imperfections, and we may battle against the idea of being a masterpiece, but we cannot deny living an extraordinary life with His Spirit within us.

What image comes to mind when you think of a masterpiece? Can you embrace your imperfections and believe this truth?

Masterpiece, you are no longer a lump of clay, so go and live an extraordinary life!

Additional Verses: Genesis 2:7; Ecclesiastes 11:5; Job 33:6; Isaiah 45:9, 64:8; Ephesians 1:13-14; 2 Corinthians 4:7

NOTES

WE ARE THE
WORK OF HIS
HAND, FORMED
AND FASHIONED
IN HIS LIKENESS
AND LOVINGLY
STAMPED WITH HIS
MAKER'S MARK.

SECURE

SEAWEED HOLDFAST

To love the Lord your God, to walk in all
His ways and to hold fast to Him.

DEUTERONOMY 11:22, NKJV

God is portrayed throughout the Old Testament as our rock. David proclaimed in Psalm 62:2 that "He is my rock and my salvation; He is my fortress, I will never be shaken." Setting your hopes and dreams on people or prosperity is an unreliable foundation of sand. If you build your home on these foundations, it will crumble under the pressures of life. God is the only secure foundation, and so we should hold on to the rock that anchors us.

Seaweed is anchored to a rock on the ocean floor by what is called a holdfast. This attachment, along with air-filled bladders, allows the massive yet flexible plant to grow as tall as a tree—reaching the sunshine that penetrates the sea's surface. With a secure holding, seaweed can thrive in a turbulent ocean and create a refuge for many sea creatures that hide from predators.

What does holding fast to God look like to you? How do you live that out?

Giant seaweed can fall prey to small, spiny sea urchins that crawl along the ocean floor in search of food. When they encounter seaweed,

*Truly he is my rock
and my salvation;
he is my fortress,
I will never be shaken.*

PSALM 62:2

they use their sharp teeth to chew off and consume the holdfasts, one by one. With the last holdfast consumed, the seaweed is released from the rock and carried off by the current. Uncontrolled by predators, urchins can destroy an entire ecosystem by turning seaweed forests into barren zones devoid of both plants and animals.

Similar to sea urchins, Satan is looking for a vulnerable area to attack so that he may destroy you little by little. Our relationships, our minds, our health, and our emotions are all battlefronts. Do not be surprised by the battle, for it is promised to all of us who call ourselves children of God. Instead, prepare for battle by girding yourself with weapons that fend off the enemy. Go into battle fully clothed and firmly cemented in God's promises to you.

Are you aware of your enemy's battle plan against you? Are you putting on the full armor of God or are you partially dressed?

Hold fast to your God because He is holding fast to you.

Additional Verse: Deuteronomy 10:20; Joshua 22:5; 1 Samuel. 2:2; Psalm 18:2, 62:2; Isaiah 26:4; Luke 6:46-49, Ephesians 6:10-18; 1 Peter 5:8

NOTES

GOD IS THE
ONLY SECURE
FOUNDATION, AND
SO WE SHOULD
HOLD ON TO THE
ROCK THAT
ANCHORS US.

MIMICRY

For we do not have a high priest who is unable to empathize with our weaknesses, but we have one who has been tempted in every way, just as we are—yet he did not sin.

HEBREWS 4:15

The Son of Man took on flesh but did not take on our sinful nature. He was tempted in every way, but He did not succumb to His humanity and the desires of the flesh. Jesus was fully God, so He was uniquely equipped to model a perfect standard for us to follow.

Mimicry in animals is a form of imitation. Some animals were created with the ability to color blend into their environment and hide from predators. Others use mimicry to entice prey by pretending to be prey themselves. And still others present warnings to predators even though they are neither poisonous nor dangerous.

Who are you following either online or in person? What about their lives attracts you?

Mockingbirds and brown thrashers are vocal mimics. These birds can repeat hundreds of learned sounds from their habitat. Amazingly, the brown thrasher can learn more than 1,000 distinct bird sounds. Mockingbirds can learn 200 sounds and are known for mimicking telephone rings, car alarms, rusty gates, and chainsaws in addition to

For I have come down from heaven not to do my will but to do the will of him who sent me.

JOHN 6:38

the bird songs in their area. These fascinating birds use their learned sounds to attract a mate and protect their territory as they repeat them over and over.

Jesus was sent to earth ultimately to rescue humanity from sin and death but also to teach us how to live. He was a leader and mentor and embraced His mission to love well. He challenged societal norms and called forth servant leaders. His ministry focused on developing relationships with men and women who learned to model His ways and live a surrendered life of obedience. Jesus demonstrated a life of prayer, faith, trust, and dependence on the Father and was the perfect example for us to follow.

Do you know Jesus well enough to mimic His ways? Are you willing to study the Scriptures to learn more about Him?

Mimicking Jesus is a practice that starts with knowledge.

Additional Verses: Luke 22:39-45; John 6:38, 10:10;
Romans 3:10-11,23; 2 Corinthians 5:21

NOTES

JESUS
DEMONSTRATED A
LIFE OF PRAYER,
FAITH, TRUST, AND
DEPENDENCE ON
THE FATHER AND
WAS THE PERFECT
EXAMPLE FOR US
TO FOLLOW.

DEPENDENCE
DESERTS

I will lead [Israel] into the wilderness and speak tenderly to her.

HOSEA 2:14

The Israelites, upon fleeing Egyptian slavery, took up residency in the desert. They realized quickly that this unfriendly land held challenges they were unprepared to handle. They fled what they had known to embrace their freedom in the unknown. Even though they witnessed many miracles surrounding their rescue, their desperate state led them to question God's motives. They feared that God had led them to the desert to die.

Desert adaptations make it possible for plants and animals to survive extreme conditions. Survival strategies include managing heat, acquiring and conserving water, and defending against predation. Plants cover their leaves with wax or hairs to prevent water loss, send roots deep or broad to collect rainfall and groundwater, and produce toxins or thorns to defend themselves. Desert animals hunt or forage at night, acquire water through their food, find refuge in burrows or desert edges, and retain water through their specialized kidneys. Desert dwellers must overcome unique challenges in order to survive.

Have you ever questioned God's leading? What were the circumstances surrounding your desert experience?

The poor and needy search for water,
but there is none;
their tongues are parched with thirst.
But I the Lord will answer them;
I, the God of Israel, will not forsake them.

ISAIAH 41:17

Brief periods of rain allow life to exist year-round in the desert. Cacti are especially suited for desert life by soaking up and storing large volumes of rainfall in their accordion-like pleats. The water is then rationed over the coming year and defended by their sharp spines. Rainfall triggers cacti and other plants to bloom and fruit, perpetuating more cacti, while also supplying food and water to support animal life.

The desert offered the Israelites distance and safety from their pursuing captors and an opportunity to begin again. God had led them away from the hardships of Egypt so that He could reestablish an Abba Father relationship with them. He removed their suffering and provided for their physical daily needs so that they could deepen their dependence on and trust in Him.

Do you resist or welcome being led into the desert? Do you recognize that the desert experiences of life have meaning and purpose?

We are promised never to be deserted by God, so instead look for the gifts that He has for you in your desert time.

Additional Verses: Exodus 16:2-4; Isaiah 41:17-20, 45:3; Mark 6:31

NOTES

WE ARE
PROMISED NEVER
TO BE DESERTED
BY GOD, SO
INSTEAD LOOK
FOR THE GIFTS
THAT HE HAS FOR
YOU IN YOUR
DESERT TIME.

COMMISSIONED
BLOOM

*Therefore go and make disciples of all nations, baptizing them
in the name of the Father and of the Son and of the Holy Spirit,
and teaching them to obey everything I have commanded you.*

MATTHEW 28:19-20

In the Great Commission, Jesus charged His disciples to go and make disciples of all nations. Leading up to this commissioning, Jesus had discipled them for years and witnessed their faith grow deeper and stronger as they lived and served together. As disciples of Christ, these men were equipped to disciple others, so upon receiving the Holy Spirit, they went.

Gardening experts readily share their knowledge with excited beginners. Gardening is a skill set learned with passion, patience, and persistence. Successful garden practices include weed removal, soil enrichment, seed dispersal, and consistent watering. Once a plant emerges from seed, the watchful caretaker tends to the vulnerable plant so that it does not wilt and die during its fragile start in life.

Why is discipleship important in developing your faith? What are the pitfalls of trying to grow alone?

Perennial plants invest in the development of roots more so than annual plants. Annuals survive for one growing season while

Follow my example,
as I follow the
example of Christ.

1 CORINTHIANS 11:1

perennials can survive for many years. By building a network of roots, the perennials withstand temperature swings and guard against drought. To encourage the growth of perennials, a gardener may apply fertilizer, protect against insects, and add stakes to support the weight of large flowers or fruited stems. Gardeners play an important role in the survival of these plants.

New believers are vulnerable to the attack of the enemy, and if left alone, their new faith can wilt or fade. Discipleship is a way that the body of Christ can encourage new believers to grow and deepen their understanding of and relationship with God. It is in relationship with one another that we all grow, support one another, and strengthen the entire body of Christ.

Have you discipled a new believer? Have you witnessed a new believer wither and walk away from the faith?

Abundant life in Christ is available to each believer, so seek it out in relationship with one another.

Additional Verses: Matthew 13:19-23; Acts 1:8;
1 Corinthians 11:1; Titus; Hebrews 10:24-25

NOTES

IT IS IN
RELATIONSHIP WITH
ONE ANOTHER
THAT WE ALL
GROW, SUPPORT
ONE ANOTHER,
AND STRENGTHEN
THE ENTIRE BODY
OF CHRIST.

KNOWN
SHEEP

My sheep listen to my voice; I know them, and they follow me.

JOHN 10:27

God uses the beauty of nature to speak to us. In the Bible, Job spoke of star constellations and was awed by God the creator and miracle worker. As Job wrestled with great loss and questioned his maker, God responded in a personal way that resonated with Job: "Can you bind the chains of the Pleiades? Can you loosen Orion's belt? Can you bring forth the constellations in their seasons or lead out the Bear with its cubs?" (Job 38:31-32). God used Job's knowledge of star constellations to reveal that He was orchestrating every detail of his life. This brought clarity to Job in his search for answers.

The close relationship between shepherd and flock is special and best understood by farming communities. Sheep survive because they listen to their shepherd, who speaks to them. He protects them from predators, safeguards them from dangers, and tends to their wounds. The shepherd leads the flock to fresh water and tender grass because he is their caretaker and their provider. The sheep listen and respond to the call of the shepherd because he is good and he does good for them.

What is God's love language to you? Do you recognize that He uniquely tends your heart because He understands you?

"I am the good shepherd; I know my
sheep and my sheep know me."

JOHN 10:14

Naturalists learn to distinguish the calls of birds and frogs so that they can teach others to identify them as well. A bullfrog will sing "jug of rum" and a chickadee will sing its name. Most wildlife animals have a unique sound, so when you learn the song or sound you don't need to see the creature to identify it.

There are many examples in the Bible of God speaking. He uses dreams, angels, prophets, and even clouds or fire to speak. He also uses simple things like a child's hug, a friend's smile, a pet's greeting, a song, a color, or a fragrance. Your spiritual eyes and ears can be trained to recognize God's messages to you. He uses your unique way of listening. If you haven't heard Him speak recently, ask and then incline your ear to hear Him. Hunt for Him where you have "seen" Him before.

When do you hear God the loudest? Is your heart searching for him?

Quiet the chaos and listen for God, because He is singing over you.

Additional Verses: Job 9:9; Psalm 23, 139:17-18; John 10:1-5,14-15; Mark 4:9

NOTES

IF YOU HAVEN'T
HEARD HIM SPEAK
RECENTLY, ASK
AND THEN INCLINE
YOUR EAR TO HEAR
HIM. HUNT FOR
HIM WHERE YOU
HAVE "SEEN"
HIM BEFORE.

ETERNAL
TEMPORAL

Do not store up for yourselves treasures on earth, where
moths and rust destroy, and where thieves break in and
steal. But store up for yourselves treasures in heaven.

MATTHEW 6:19-20 NASB

Moths, rust, and thieves are a few of the forces that work against our ability to accumulate wealth on earth. All three were and still are difficult to control. It is natural to be consumed with the temporary, the earthly, and the needs of the day. Jesus challenged His listeners to redirect their short-sighted focus toward treasures that cannot be stolen or destroyed.

Everything we see, taste, and touch is temporary. Clothes moths, rust, and thieves ensure that our possessions are transitory. In order to survive, clothes moth larvae consume and destroy clothing and fabric made with natural fibers. Rust, or iron oxide, is another destructive force that will attack and consume metal. In the presence of water, metal corrodes, flakes, and disintegrates. Thieves, instead of destroying property, will remove others' gains and claim possession as they attempt to build their own stockpile.

What do you treasure? Do your time and talent investments reflect that?

Bring the whole tithe into the storehouse, that there may be food in my house. Test me in this," says the Lord Almighty, "and see if I will not throw open the floodgates of heaven and pour out so much blessing that there will not be room enough to store it.

MALACHI 3:10

It is difficult to preserve and protect any accumulation. Tiny destroyers such as bacteria and fungi are always at work, turning our food moldy and decomposing dead trees and animals. Their abundant spores fill the air we breathe and turn everything living back into soil.

Fear of the future motivates us to store wealth. In Matthew 6, Jesus assures us that this fear is unfounded because we have a God who provides all we need. We are encouraged to seek first His kingdom and His righteousness above all earthly goals and ambitions. He is our Jehovah Jireh and will provide for our futures.

Does your fear of the future limit your eternal investments? If you were to dream big for the kingdom, where would you give without reservation?

Consider Malachi 3:10 as God's promise that He will outgive your obedience and offerings to Him, so don't hold back!

Additional Verses: Malachi 3:10; Proverbs 8:17-21;
Matthew 6:21,31-33, 13:44-46; 1 John 2:17

NOTES

HE IS OUR

JEHOVAH JIREH

AND WILL

PROVIDE FOR

OUR FUTURES.

HOLINESS
DEFENSES

Taste and see that the Lord is good.

PSALM 34:8

On Mt. Sinai, God gave guardrails to Moses to help the wandering Israelites from wandering off into the "briars" of life. His Ten Commandments focused on their relationships with God and with their community. God gave these guidelines so that His chosen people would be holy, healthy, and a nation preserved for generations to come.

It is wise to consider and heed warning signs. Plants that are armed and ready for battle often post warnings and have strategies to inflict pain on would-be consumers and accidental stumblers. Thorns and spines act as armor to prevent the hungry animal from reaching the fleshy plant. Oils, acids, and poisons are a plant's chemical warfare to cause stomach aches, itchy and irritated skin, and sometimes even death. These plants defend their right to live in their rooted location.

Do you tend to be a rule-follower or do you rebel against rules? How has your stance on life worked for or against you?

When animals eat toxic plants, they initially get an upset stomach. If an animal is eating slowly enough, its stomach will signal its brain to stop consuming the plant. Some animals have limited food options and are unable to avoid toxic plants, so instead they consume clay,

One who is full loathes
honey from the comb, but
to the hungry even what
is bitter tastes sweet.

PROVERBS 27:7

which binds and removes the toxins, preventing absorption into their blood. However, animals that overconsume toxins or accidentally ingest poisons often die because they are unable to reverse the effects.

Veering from God's commandments often brings consequences. Jesus told us to be holy as He is holy, which means that it is possible to live a life separate from the world. Choosing poorly or rebelling against God's plan for you will give you more than a belly ache; it will bring a heart sickness that cannot be healed with medicine. God's rules are meant for your good and to prevent pain from being a part of your story. What appears at first glance to be honey may actually be toxic to your soul.

Where have you veered in the past from God's best plan? Do you still question God's forgiveness or wrestle with offering yourself forgiveness?

You are chosen, sanctified, consecrated, and set apart to be His.

Additional Verses: Deuteronomy 5:6-21,29, 6:5-9; Proverbs 27:7; Romans 1:1; 1 Peter 1:16

NOTES

YOU ARE CHOSEN,
SANCTIFIED,
CONSECRATED,
AND SET APART
TO BE HIS.

BIRD DESIGN

For you created my inmost being; you knit me
together in my mother's womb. I praise you because
I am fearfully and wonderfully made.

PSALM 139:13-14

God the artist has created you to uniquely reflect His own image. He formed you with intention so that your physical features and your gifts would amaze others and remind them of your creative Father. You were not made to compete with others but to complement them and reflect your uniqueness to them.

All of creation showcases God's artistry. Birds are unique in the animal kingdom because most of them fly. Within the class of birds, we can identify so many by their beautiful and noticeable variations in size, shape, and color. Other features such as beaks, feet, eggs, nests, and behavior require a closer look to see how those features distinguish them from each other.

What makes you uniquely you? As a reflection of God, what does your uniqueness reveal about your Father?

Bird beaks were given to birds not just as an attachment to their head but also as a tool for acquiring food. Some beaks are designed for opening seeds, others for drilling dead wood to find insects, piercing

to equip his people for works of service, so that the body of Christ may be built up.

EPHESIANS 4:12

and tearing prey, or collecting nectar. These beaks were designed for each bird's good.

God has also given you tools or gifts in your mother's womb. When you walk in faith and in step with the Lord, He unveils hidden treasures within you. Personality and spiritual gift inventories can reveal insight into the way God has made you unique. God gave us each a tool, a gift, and a job to encourage and strengthen the whole. He did not give us all the same gift, because He had designed us to work together as it says in Ephesians 4:12—"so that the body of Christ may be built up." We were designed to glorify God by using our complementary gifts so that in turn we would strengthen the worldwide Church.

In what ways are you partnering with God by using the gifts He has given you? Have you felt the gentle nudge of the Lord to be involved in a new, and maybe uncomfortable, area of ministry?

Use your unique way of revealing God's heart to others by pushing fear out of your path.

Additional Verses: Ephesians 4:11-13, 1 Corinthians 12:1-31

NOTES

GOD THE
ARTIST HAS
CREATED YOU
TO UNIQUELY
REFLECT HIS
OWN IMAGE.

REVELATION
CREATED
COMPLEXITY

For since the creation of the world God's invisible
qualities—his eternal power and divine nature—have
been clearly seen, being understood from what has
been made, so that people are without excuse.

ROMANS 1:20

David in Psalm 19 revels in the beauty of the heavens as he eloquently proclaims that no words are needed to understand their language. God's vastness is captured in the planets that orbit the sun, star constellations that constantly shine, sunsets with incredible colors, and the changing phases of the moon. God created this universal message board so that man would know He exists. Being a member of this world gives you a special insight into its designer because He has created and is still creating.

Design and order exist in the natural world and can be seen in plants, animals, man, and in how systems function. There is beauty and complexity all around us. The more you look and learn, the more you understand and see how incredibly everything works together.

When was the last time you watched a sunrise or sunset with awe? What systems in nature have drawn your attention lately?

The heavens declare the glory of God;
the skies proclaim the work of his hands.

PSALM 19:1

Scientists are still discovering all kinds of life under a microscope, in the deepest oceans, in hidden caves, and in the rainforests. Stars and galaxies unknown are now being reached by new telescopes. For thousands of years, these species and stars have existed without our knowledge.

In Amos 4 and 5, Amos reminds the Israelites about God's active involvement in His creation. God forms mountains, creates wind, turns night to day, calls ocean water, pours rain, treads the heights of the earth and reveals His thoughts to man. God not only created this world for us, He created this world and an endless universe for His glory. He desires that we would see and hear Him through His creation and in turn praise Him, not only for His mighty works, but for who He is.

How does God's creative heart draw you into a deeper relationship with Him? How does God use His creation to communicate to you in a personal way?

Step outside, look up, and connect with the eternal God tonight.

Additional Verses: Job 26:7-14; Psalm 19:1-6; Ecclesiastes 3:11; Amos 4:13, 5:8; Romans 1:18,19

NOTES

GOD NOT ONLY
CREATED THIS
WORLD FOR US,
HE CREATED THIS
WORLD AND AN
ENDLESS UNIVERSE
FOR HIS GLORY.

PLANTED TREE

Blessed is the one who trusts in the Lord, whose confidence is in him. They will be like a tree planted by the water that sends out its roots by the stream. It does not fear when heat comes; its leaves are always green. It has no worries in a year of drought and never fails to bear fruit.

JEREMIAH 17:7-8

You are a tree that has been purposely planted near water. God's intention is to grow your faith and your trust in Him as you recognize that He is your strength, your salvation, and your hope. He will grow spiritual fruit that is birthed from His relationship with you. When you feel as if you could wither and die, He will be the one that gives refreshment and strength so that you can stand, no matter what comes.

Drought stress is often the demise of a transplanted tree. Trees that are dug for transport have severed roots and experience shock which makes it difficult to survive in their new location without care. Urban foresters will provide a consistent watering schedule to help the newly planted trees overcome root damage and combat other city stressors such as pollution, amplified heat, and soil compaction. Trees planted near a water source have an advantage that most city trees

Many, Lord my God,
are the wonders
you have done,
the things you
planned for us.
None can compare
with you;
were I to speak and
tell of your deeds,
they would be too
many to declare.

PSALM 40:5

do not. Their position greatly increases their chance of survival and their ability to flourish throughout the coming years.

Do you trust in God's plan? Do your words and thoughts reflect that trust?

Most tree species would grow well near a water source. Some trees even thrive in waterlogged soils. These trees are considered wetland indicators because they help experts deduce the presence of water at or near the ground surface. Many trees that naturally grow in or near a stream, pond, or swamp would not survive on a dry site for very long.

Surrendering to God's plans allows you to live an abundant life. Confidence and contentment replace fear and anxiety when you recognize you have a constant source of nourishment. God has planted you where you are, with your circumstances, and in relationship with those around you.

Is your abundant life on display and recognizable from a distance? Who has God used to grow your faith and deepen your connection to the Father?

Trust that God is the one orchestrating your growth.

Additional Verses: Psalm 1:1-3, 40:5; Isaiah 58:11, 61:1-3

NOTES

DO YOU TRUST
IN GOD'S PLAN?
DO YOUR WORDS
AND THOUGHTS
REFLECT THAT
TRUST?

ADOPTED

BROWN-HEADED COWBIRD

For you did not receive the spirit of slavery to fall
back into fear, but you have received the Spirit of
adoption as sons, by whom we cry, "Abba! Father!"

ROMANS 8:15, ESV

Many families have opened their hearts and homes to children who are not their own. Jesus opened the adoption doors to those of us without a Jewish heritage through His death and resurrection. Instead of being abandoned, we have been chosen, accepted, and welcomed into the family as sons and daughters of the Most High God and co-heirs with Christ. Confirmation of this adoption comes from the Holy Spirit, and we are called to live in the security of our new name.

Animals have been known to adopt species like or unlike themselves. Birds that force adoption on other birds are called brood parasites. The brown-headed cowbird is a brood parasite found in North America. Instead of building a nest, she will consume or push out an egg from an existing nest and replace it with her own. The nest builder will incubate the foreign egg and feed the demanding hatchling, despite it growing to twice her size. Similarly, in Europe,

The Lord himself
goes before you and
will be with you; he
will never leave you
nor forsake you. Do
not be afraid; do not
be discouraged.

DEUTERONOMY 31:8

the common cuckoo's hatchling, often laid in a small nest, will fill the space and push the other eggs and hatchlings out prematurely. Despite this tragic end, the adoptive mother does not abandon the young cuckoo.

Have you surrendered your life to God? What does freedom in Christ afford you?

The warbler mother can adopt and accept the burden of raising an abandoned cowbird egg or she can reject the entire group of eggs in her nest. Experienced mothers may build a nest in a new location or construct another nest layer to cover the cold abandoned eggs. In her persistence to mother, she will lay a clutch of eggs in her new nest, in hopes that another foreign egg will not appear.

God promises never to leave us or forsake us. Our adoption is binding—secure and forever. Our Abba Father's arms are open to us, and we can approach and embrace Him as we would a loving earthly father.

Do you sense God's great love for you as His beloved child? Do you find it more difficult to grasp God's kingly majesty or His fatherly tenderness?

As a child of the King, you have been given a new name, a royal heritage, a hope, and a future, so go live in the abundance of His love and acceptance of you.

Additional Verses: Deuteronomy 31:8; John 10:14; Galatians 4:4-7; Ephesians 1:3-6,11-12, 2:19; Philippians 3:20-21

NOTES

GOD PROMISES

NEVER TO

LEAVE US OR

FORSAKE US.

THIRST
ESSENTIAL TO LIFE

Let anyone who is thirsty come to me and drink.
Whoever believes in me, as Scripture has said, rivers
of living water will flow from within them.

JOHN 7:37-38

Though all plants and animals thirst for the combination of hydrogen and oxygen known as water, man is the only one who also thirsts for living water. We are invited with a promise that when we drink living water, we will be filled. The phrase, *Let anyone who is thirsty* seems to imply that some are thirsty and others are not. In truth, all are thirsty, but not all recognize that their thirst is for God. It is often easier to identify our need for food and water because of the signals from our physical body than it is to recognize our daily need for God.

Without water, plant and animal cells dehydrate and die. A plant with ample water will thrive, generating more flowers, fruit, and brilliant fall leaf colors. Inversely, drought causes stunted growth, few if any flowers and fruit, and a lackluster fall leaf display.

What red flags in your behavior or thought patterns reveal that your soul is parched? Do you recognize that a worried mind, an anxious heart, or a grumbling spirit is the cry of a parched soul?

The thief comes only to steal and kill
and destroy; I have come that they may
have life, and have it to the full.

JOHN 10:10

Both plants and animals adjust during periods of drought. Plants can temporarily wilt or flip their leaves to reveal a white reflective underside—slowing photosynthesis and reducing their consumption of water. Animals will adjust their normal behavior and rest during the heat to prevent dehydration. By limiting their activity to dawn and dusk when the sun is less intense, they reduce their need for water.

Recognizing that your soul is parched is critical for change. Jesus said in John 10:10 that He came to bring life, abundant life. This life is not focused on the self-gratification the world offers; instead it is a life rich with meaning, relationships, and joy.

Where are you seeking refreshment for your soul? What, if anything, needs to change?

Stop settling for substitutes and choose the abundant life that is yours through Christ.

Additional Verses: Job 14:7-9; Psalm 23:2-3, 42:1, 107:8-9;
Matthew 5:6; John 4:13-14; Revelation 21:6

NOTES

STOP SETTLING
FOR SUBSTITUTES
AND CHOOSE
THE ABUNDANT
LIFE THAT IS
YOURS THROUGH
CHRIST.

TRANSFORMATION
CHANGING
SEASONS

He who began a good work in you
will carry it on to completion until
the day of Christ Jesus.

PHILIPPIANS 1:6

Each chapter of our story may be filled with changes that provide hope and hardship simultaneously. A change could mean possibilities and adventure but also the loss of community connections. Grief often accompanies change but provides an opportunity for transformation. God can use our vulnerability to do inward work in our hearts, leading to an outward beauty that is otherworldly.

Beautiful fall leaf colors inspire a road trip to the woods. As the Earth tilts away from the sun, daylight shortens in length and trees begin their preparation for winter—halting the production of green chlorophyll to unveil the hidden yellow and orange pigments. Red, blue, and purple pigments are created as the sun stimulates the stored sugar in the leaf. Trees that store more residual sugar in their leaves undergo a chemical reaction fueled by the sun that converts the sugar into a brilliant display of color as seen in oak, maple, and sweetgum trees.

There is a time for
everything, and a
season for every activity
under the heavens

ECCLESIASTES 3:1

When have you experienced both joy and grief during a period of change? Did your sadness propel you to seek out God and others or did you turn inward to try to protect your pain?

Leaves that are shaded by upper branches or by other trees can turn directly from green to brown and then fall from the tree unnoticed. They do not turn brilliant colors, nor are they transformed by the sun. Though the tree ceases chlorophyll production in every leaf, the individual leaf outcome differs. Some are beautiful and some are not. The trees have no control over which leaves are made beautiful by the sun.

Unlike the tree, we have an opportunity to respond. Our faith and dependence on God are put to the test during times of uncertainty and change. Some transformations are instantaneous, but most take time and patience.

When have you experienced a loss that later became the room needed for growth? Have you been able to reflect and appreciate the gift despite the sting of loss?

He has promised to complete the good work He has started in you.

Additional Verses: Ecclesiastes 3:1-8; Ezekiel 36:26; 2 Corinthians 5:17

NOTES

HE HAS PROMISED
TO COMPLETE
THE GOOD
WORK HE HAS
STARTED IN YOU.

WHOLE SELF
LICHEN

We are confident, I say, and would prefer to be away
from the body and at home with the Lord.

2 CORINTHIANS 5:8

We are both temporal and eternal. Our body is made from the dust of the earth, our soul is composed of our mind, emotions, and will, and our spirit is our connection to eternity. This interesting relationship allows our temporal frame to house our eternal self. At the end of our time on earth, our bodies will remain, but our soul and spirit will continue.

Symbiotic, or mutually beneficial relationships in nature were first discovered in the 19th century. Lichen is an organism that is composed of a symbiotic relationship between algae and fungi. Algae, often found in water, and fungi, often found in the forest grow in different habitats and seem to be unlikely partners. Mysteriously, they can together form lichen and grow nearly anywhere by sharing the algae's photosynthetic food and using the fungi's ability to collect water and nutrients. Much like how our body and mind come together to create us.

Which are you more likely to neglect: your aging body or your eternal soul? What self care practices need to be added to address your neglect?

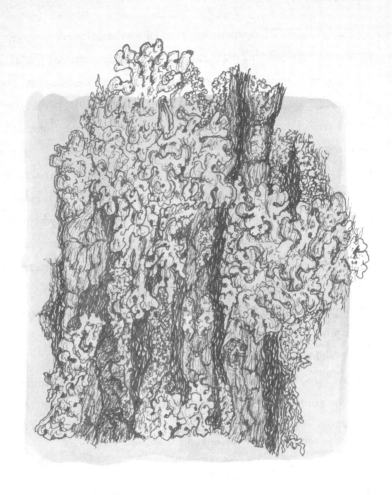

Because through Christ Jesus the law of the Spirit who gives

life has set you[a] free from the law of sin and death.

ROMANS 8:2

Though lichen has been the focus of studies, the relationship formation between this plant (algae) and this decomposer (fungi) is a mystery. Scientists still harvest lichen samples from the field for study, because they have not yet successfully bonded the two in the lab. Mysteries are what drive scientists to ask more questions and continue to research.

The relationship between our temporal body and our eternal soul and spirit is a mystery to us as Christians even though God revealed it to us. Our spirit is promised a place with Him forever when we surrender our minds, heart, and will to the lordship of Christ. Your current body will be left on earth, but your spirit will spend eternity with Him in a promised new body that will never waste away.

What words would best describe your current legacy? What descriptors would you want added and what would you need to change to be remembered that way?

Saved from this life for the next, you are a complex and beautiful being on your way to an eternity with God.

Additional Verses: Proverbs 31:30; Matthew 10:28, 16:26;
Romans 8:2; 2 Corinthians 4:16; 1 Thessalonians 5:23

NOTES

AT THE END OF

OUR TIME ON

EARTH, OUR

BODIES WILL

REMAIN, BUT

OUR SOUL AND

SPIRIT WILL

CONTINUE.

ABOUT THE AUTHOR

JILL SMITH is a writer and speaker with a deep love for nature. She earned her BS in environmental biology from Taylor University and her MS in natural resources from Ball State University. She moved to Nashville, Tennessee, with her husband and worked as a forester at Warner Parks, one of the country's largest city parks. While there she managed fields and forests, wrote articles for *Wildland Weeds* and the *Tennessee Conservationist*, and developed educational programs for children and adults.

After leaving forestry and becoming a full-time mother, Jill began journaling about the connections between Scripture and creation. She returned to forestry as the executive director of the Tennessee Urban Forestry Council and helped spread tree education throughout Tennessee by developing community arboreta. When not writing and speaking, Jill loves to hike, walk dogs, work in her garden, and help others ditch chemical cleaning with her Norwex business. She lives in Nashville with her husband and two teenage sons.

Connect with Jill at
https://jillsmith.my.canva.site/life-long-learner

Growing up in a small lake town in upstate New York, **STACEY BARR** found her love for nature, art, and Jesus. Drawing from these joys she pursued art school, where she partook in many of the fine arts, majoring in painting while also enjoying art history, printmaking, and especially drawing. She began that journey at SUNY Cortland and completed her BS in studio art at The College of St. Rose, where she also completed classes in art education and graphic design. With art always in her heart, she pursued it wherever she was, painting murals, creating logo designs, and drawing commissioned pieces. While living in Maine she began an art school for K-12 homeschool students that continued and grew even with her transition to Tennessee. She was invited to begin an art club and curate an art gallery at her church in Tennessee, as well as complete her own God-inspired pastel drawings during productions and musical worship sessions. Her dream to illustrate a book, starting in seventh grade, is being realized here with this book, even as she continues with other illustrating requests. Stacey now resides on sixteen acres in Chapel Hill, where her amazing husband and four beautiful children are surrounded and inspired by God's creation daily.

ACKNOWLEDGEMENTS

A sense of wonder, a long list of teachers, professors, and colleagues, and a God who speaks in the silence—these are why this book is in print. I'm grateful for the many people who have encouraged my curiosity of God and nature and have spent time nurturing those interests. For those who have invested in this project in the form of both science and content edits, thank you for challenging my ideas and helping me to communicate them better. To Stacey Barr, my friend and rockstar illustrator, thank you for creating such beautiful images to amplify the devotion stories. Bravo, friend! Thank you to my loving and supportive friends and family who have blown wind into my sails. My life is richer because of you! Lastly, to Gary Smith, you are my favorite! I'm so grateful to God for our love story and that it is still being written.

NOTES

NOTES